Spooky Spots

SPOOKY HISTORICAL SITES

SCOTT WILKEN

Big Buddy Books

An Imprint of Abdo Publishing
abdobooks.com

abdobooks.com

Published by Abdo Publishing, a division of ABDO, PO Box 398166, Minneapolis, Minnesota 55439.

Printed in China
052020
092020

Design: Sarah DeYoung, Mighty Media, Inc.
Production: Mighty Media, Inc.
Editor: Liz Salzmann

Cover Photograph: Shutterstock Images
Interior Photographs: Ebyabe/Wikimedia Commons, pp. 6 (Old St. Johns County Jail), 23; Shutterstock Images, pp. 4–5, 6, 7 (all), 9, 10–11, 13, 14–15, 17, 18, 21, 25, 26–27, 28 (all), 29 (all); Wikimedia Commons, p. 19
Design Elements: Shutterstock Images

Library of Congress Control Number: 2020931737

Publisher's Cataloging-in-Publication Data
Names: Wilken, Scott, author.
Title: Spooky historical sites / by Scott Wilken
Description: Minneapolis, Minnesota : Abdo Publishing, 2021 | Series: Spooky spots | Includes online resources and index
Identifiers: ISBN 9781532193330 (lib. bdg.) | ISBN 9781098211974 (ebook)
Subjects: LCSH: Haunted places--Juvenile literature. | Ghosts--Juvenile literature. | Historic sites--Juvenile literature. | Spirits--Juvenile literature.
Classification: DDC 133.12--dc23

CONTENTS

HAUNTED HISTORICAL SITES

Do you believe there are ghosts among us? Many people do. Whether you're a believer or not, historical **sites** are some of the spookiest spots around!

Get ready to **explore** some of the most haunted historical sites on Earth. Walk along the walls of ancient **forts**. Visit dark cells in old prisons. But look out! You may not be alone.

Many people believe that the older a place is, the more likely it is to be haunted.

World's Spookiest
HISTORICAL SITES

Are you ready for a ghostly adventure? Then pack up your wits and your **courage**. Let's take a trip to some of the world's spookiest historical **sites**!

The Tower of London, England
Lawang Sewu, Indonesia
Bhangarh Fort, India
Port Arthur, Australia
RUSSIA
INDIA
AUSTRALIA
Indian Ocean
South Atlantic Ocean
N
S
E
W
ICELAND
NORWAY
GERMANY
POLAND
UKRAINE
FRANCE
SPAIN
PORTUGAL
ITALY
ROMANIA
TURKEY
SYRIA
KAZAKHSTAN
AFGHANISTAN
PAKISTAN
NEPAL
MOROCCO
ALGERIA
MAURITANIA
MALI
NIGER
CHAD
NIGERIA
GUINEA
KENYA
TANZANIA
DEMOCRATIC REPUBLIC OF THE CONGO
GABON
ANGOLA
ZAMBIA
NAMIBIA
BOTSWANA
ZIMBABWE
SOUTH AFRICA
MADAGASCAR
SRI LANKA
THAILAND
VIETNAM
PHILIPPINES
INDONESIA
PAPUA NEW GUINEA
TIMOR LESTE
JAPAN
NORTH KOREA

THE ALAMO

The state of Texas wasn't always US territory. The land was first a part of Mexico. In 1836, Texas fought a war with Mexico to become independent.

In March that year, Mexican troops attacked the Alamo building in San Antonio, Texas. Around 185 Texans fought to **defend** the Alamo. They were all killed.

After the battle, Mexican leaders wanted to destroy the Alamo. But the men sent to do it refused. They said the **mission** was guarded by ghosts with flaming swords!

The Alamo was built by monks in the early 1700s. It was originally called Mission San Antonio de Valero.

Since the Battle of the Alamo, there have been many ghostly sightings at the **mission**. Some people have reported seeing soldiers marching in front of it. Others have heard loud moans inside the mission.

One common Alamo sighting is the ghost of a young boy. According to **legend**, the boy was sent to safety before the Battle of the Alamo. But his parents died there. So, people believe his ghost haunts the place where he last saw them.

The ghost of the young boy is usually seen in an upstairs window of the Alamo. The area is now a gift shop.

SALEM, MASSACHUSETTS

In the 1690s, more than 200 people in Salem were **accused** of witchcraft. Nineteen were hanged. Several others died in prison. The town is thought to be haunted by those who died.

Many locations around Salem have had spooky occurrences. One of these is the Old Burying Point Cemetery. Judge John Hathorne is buried there.

Hathorne sentenced some of the accused witches to death. Visitors have taken pictures of a shadowy figure near his grave. Could it be Hathorne's ghost?

The Old Burying Point Cemetery is also known as the Charter Street Cemetery. It is one of the oldest cemeteries in the United States.

Jonathan Corwin was another witch **trial** judge in old Salem. His home, Corwin House, is Salem's only remaining building from the time of the witch trials.

Corwin's ghost and the ghosts of the people he sentenced are said to haunt the house. Visitors have seen ghostly figures and felt cold spots in the building.

Corwin House is also known as the Witch House.

THE TOWER OF LONDON

The Tower of London is a **fortress** in London, England. The first part of it was built in 1078. The Tower has had many uses. These include being a royal palace, a zoo, and more.

But for 800 years, the Tower of London served as a prison. Many prisoners were held in the Tower. Some of these prisoners were kings, queens, and princes.

In April 1483, Prince Edward became king of England at the age of 12. Soon after, he and his younger brother, Prince Richard, were moved to the tower. But, by the end of the year the two boys had disappeared.

The oldest part of the Tower of London is the White Tower.

Visitors to the Tower today have seen ghostly figures of two boys wearing nightshirts. The princes were also spotted playing on the **battlements**. Some people claim to have heard children giggling!

FRIGHTFUL FACT

One famous royal prisoner was Queen Anne Boleyn. She was **beheaded** at the Tower in May 1536. Boleyn's headless ghost has since been seen wandering the halls of the **fortress**.

Some people believe that Edward and Richard's uncle, Richard, Duke of Gloucester, ordered his nephews be killed so he could be king of England.

BHANGARH FORT

Bhangarh **Fort** was built in India in the 1600s. But it soon fell into ruin. One **legend** about how this happened is about an evil wizard.

The wizard tried to give a woman who lived at the fort a **potion** to make her love him. But she threw the potion on a rock. The rock then rolled over the wizard and killed him. As he died, he cursed the fort.

Today, there are stories of strange sounds in the fort. Mysterious accidents are said to happen there.

FRIGHTFUL FACT

Visitors are not allowed to enter Bhangarh Fort after dark. Local people warn that if you go in, you may not come out!

There is a deserted village near Bhangarh Fort. It is said that if anyone tries to build a house in the village, it will fall down on its own.

OLD ST. JOHNS COUNTY JAIL

The Old St. Johns County Jail was built in St. Augustine, Florida, in 1891. It was in use until 1953.

Eight prisoners were hanged there for their crimes. Many others died from harsh conditions. Prisoners had only thin **mattresses** to sleep on and very little food to eat.

The jail is now a museum. Visitors report hearing crying, screams of pain, mad laughter, and dogs barking. Some have seen strange balls of light and ghostly figures. Some even say they felt something unseen touch them!

In 1987, the Old St. Johns County Jail was added to the US National Register of Historic Places.

PORT ARTHUR

Port Arthur was a **penal** colony in Australia. It was established by the British in 1830. At the time, the British government sent criminals to Australia as punishment for their crimes.

Those who then committed crimes in Australia were held at Port Arthur. Prisoners lived in underground cells and worked in coal mines. More than 1,600 prisoners died at the prison.

Port Arthur is now a **tourist site**. Visitors have reported strange activity there. Some suddenly felt sad, scared, or angry. Others reported seeing the ghosts of prisoners and guards.

More than 250,000 people visit Port Arthur each year.

LAWANG SEWU

Lawang Sewu in Indonesia was built in the early 1900s. It was the main office of the Dutch East Indies Railway Company.

The Japanese took over the building during **World War II**. They used it as a prison. Some prisoners were **tortured** and killed at the prison. Visitors report seeing their headless spirits wandering the halls!

FRIGHTFUL FACT

People have also reported seeing a vampire ghost at Lawang Sewu. These ghosts are called *Kuntilanak*.

Lawang Sewu means "one thousand doors" in Javanese.

SPOOKY OR SCIENCE?

You've just learned about some spooky historical **sites**. The creepy stories are fun! But good **explorers** look for reasons for what they see and hear. Strange happenings can often be explained by science.

Do you think the historical sites in this book are actually haunted? You might have to visit them to find out!

IMAGINATION

Humans have excellent imaginations. Just hearing about a scary sight can trick your brain into thinking you've seen it too!

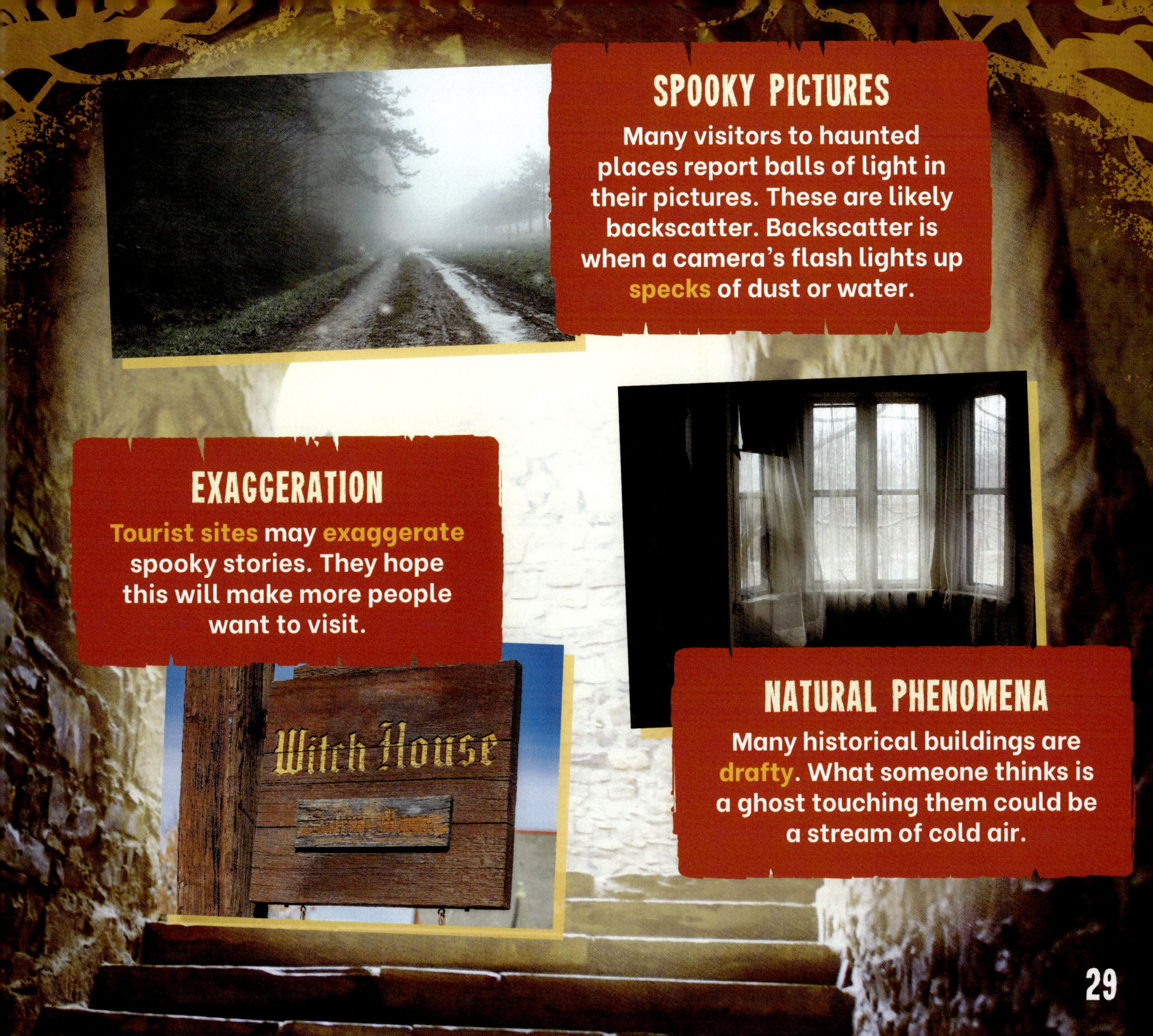

SPOOKY PICTURES

Many visitors to haunted places report balls of light in their pictures. These are likely backscatter. Backscatter is when a camera's flash lights up **specks** of dust or water.

EXAGGERATION

Tourist sites may **exaggerate** spooky stories. They hope this will make more people want to visit.

NATURAL PHENOMENA

Many historical buildings are **drafty**. What someone thinks is a ghost touching them could be a stream of cold air.

GLOSSARY

accuse – to say someone did something wrong or illegal.

battlement – a wall on top of a castle that has open spaces for soldiers to shoot through.

behead – to cut off someone's head.

courage – strength or bravery.

defend – to protect from harm or attack.

drafty – the condition of having a stream of cold air moving through a building or room.

exaggerate (ihg-ZA-juh-rayt) – to make something seem larger or more impressive.

explore – to go into in order to make a discovery or to have an adventure. A person who explores is an explorer.

fort – a strong building or group of buildings where soldiers live.

fortress – a building or town with strong walls to guard against enemies.

legend – an old story that many people believe but cannot be proven true.

mattress – a large pad that you sleep on.

mission – a place where religious work is done.

penal – relating to or used for punishment.

potion – liquids mixed together to make a medicine or poison.

site – a location.

speck – a tiny dot or particle.

torture – to purposely cause great pain and suffering to someone.

tourist site – a place people visit while on vacation.

trial – a meeting before a judge to find out whether someone did something wrong or illegal.

vampire – a made-up monster that is a dead person who comes out at night to suck the blood of living people.

World War II – a war fought in Europe, Asia, and Africa from 1939 to 1945.

ONLINE RESOURCES

To learn more about spooky historical sites, please visit **abdobooklinks.com** or scan this QR code. These links are routinely monitored and updated to provide the most current information available.

INDEX